HOW TO DRAW POSES IN FASHION
COMMENT DESSINER LES POSES DU MONDE DE LA MODE
MODEFIGURINE ZEICHNEN
POSES UIT DE MODE LEREN TEKENEN

© 2011 **booQs** publishers bvba
Godefriduskaai 22
2000 Antwerp
Belgium
Tel: + 32 3 226 66 73
Fax: + 32 3 226 53 65
www.booqs.be
info@booqs.be

ISBN: 978-94-60650-51-2
WD: D/2011/11978/03
Q076

Illustrations: Chidy Wayne
Texts: Chidy Wayne, Natalio Martín Arroyo
Art direction: Mireia Casanovas Soley
Layout: Maira Purman
Translation: Cillero & de Motta

Editorial project:
maomao publications
Via Laietana, 32, 4.º, of. 104
08003 Barcelona, Spain
Tel.: +34 932 688 088
Fax: +34 933 174 208
maomao@maomaopublications.com
www.maomaopublications.com

Printed in China

HOW TO DRAW POSES IN FASHION
COMMENT DESSINER LES POSES DU MONDE DE LA MODE
MODEFIGURINE ZEICHNEN
POSES UIT DE MODE LEREN TEKENEN

booQs

Introduction

Back in the 19th century, Parisian fashion houses hired artists to make stylized silhouettes that provided aristocrats with a representation of the gown that the couturier would be making up for a ball or reception. In modern times, fashion illustration has become a form of artistic expression with a multitude of practical and decorative functions that are increasingly in demand.

By definition, *pose* is a French word that refers to an assumed or unnatural posture. Although fashion does in fact have a particular feel of dramatism and artificality, it is not always necessary to turn to exaggeration and extreme stylization. In certain cases, fashion illustration requires a more natural and functional look, such as when depicting the realistic way a garment behaves or in order to connect the drawing with a specific style. For this reason, we bring the word *pose* together with *posture*, from the Latin word *positura*, which makes reference to the action or situation. For you to choose the right pose or posture, it is important that you consider factors like the style of clothes the model is going to wear, in order to achieve a sense of intention and attitude. We have created three chapters that show you urban, casual, and formal styles, respectively, together with hints, poses and key garments that will help you to represent them: simple outlines and watercolor tints to breathe life into your best designs.

Introduction

Au 19e siècle, les maisons de haute couture parisienne sollicitaient déjà les services d'artistes qui, grâce à leurs silhouettes stylisées, montraient aux aristocrates la future robe de soirée que le maître confectionnerait pour un bal ou une réception. De nos jours, l'illustration de la mode est devenue une forme d'expression artistique de plus en plus sollicitée, avec de nombreuses fonctions pratiques et ornementales.

Le mot « pose » se rapporte au fait de prendre une attitude peu naturelle. En effet, la mode a ce côté mélodramatique et factice, sans qu'il soit pour autant nécessaire de tomber dans l'exagération et la stylisation extrême. Dans certains cadres, l'illustration de mode exige un style plus naturel et fonctionnel, par exemple pour exprimer l'allure réaliste d'un vêtement ou pour assimiler le dessin à un style précis. Pour cela nous confrontons le mot *pose* à celui de *position*, qui provient du latin *positura* et fait allusion à l'action ou la situation. Au moment de choisir la pose ou la position appropriée, il est important d'avoir en tête des facteurs comme le style de vêtement que portera le mannequin afin de capter l'intention et l'attitude. Cet ouvrage comporte trois chapitres qui reflètent le style urbain, le style *casual* et le style formel. Vous y trouverez des astuces, les poses et les vêtements clés qui vous aideront à les représenter: des trais simples et des voiles en aquarelle pour donner vie à vos meilleurs designs.

Vorwort

Schon im XIX. Jahrhundert stellten die Pariser Haute Couture-Häuser Künstler ein, die den Aristokraten mit Hilfe von stilisierten Silhouetten eine Vorstellung davon gaben, wie ein Festkleid, das der Meister für einen Ball oder einen Empfang schneidern sollte, aussehen würde. Heutzutage hat sich die Modezeichnung zu einer Kunstrichtung gewandelt, die mit ihren vielfältigen praktischen und dekorativen Funktionen immer mehr gefragt wird.

Definitionsgemäß bezieht sich das Wort *Pose*, das aus dem Französischen *pose* kommt, auf eine natürliche Körperhaltung. Tatsächlich gibt es in der Mode diesen dramatischen und künstlichen Aspekt, aber Übertreibung und extremen Stilisierung sind nicht immer sinnvoll. In bestimmten Bereichen wird von der Modezeichnung mehr Natürlichkeit und Funktionalität verlangt; z.B., um das realistische Verhalten eines Kleidungsstücks zu demonstrieren oder um durch die Zeichnung einen konkreten Stil zu kennzeichnen. Aus diesem Grund vergleichen wir das Wort *Pose* mit dem lateinischen *Positur*, das auf eine Handlung oder Situation anspielt. Um die korrekte Pose oder Positur zu wählen, ist es wichtig, Faktoren wie den Kleidungsstil, den das Model tragen wird, einzubeziehen, um Intension und Verhalten zu verdeutlichen. So zeigen wir in drei Kapiteln den urbanen, den *casual* und den formellen Stil, neben Tricks, Posen und Kleidungsstücken, die eine Schlüsselrolle spielen, und die helfen, diese Stile darzustellen: mit einfachen Strichen und Aquarellfarben, um Ihren besten Designs Leben zu verleihen.

Inleiding

Al in de 19de eeuw trokken de Parijse haute-couturezaken kunstenaars aan die, door middel van stijlvolle silhouetten, de aristocraten een voorstelling lieten zien van hoe de feestkleding die de ontwerper voor een dansavond of receptie zou maken eruit zou zien. Tegenwoordig is de mode-illustratie uitgegroeid tot een uiting van kunst, met talrijke praktische en decoratieve functies, waar steeds meer vraag naar is.

Het woord *pose* komt van het Franse *pose*, en verwijst naar een vrij onnatuurlijke lichaamshouding. De mode heeft inderdaad iets dramatisch en kunstmatigs, maar het is niet altijd nodig om in overdrijving en extreme stilering te vervallen. In bepaalde kringen vereist de mode-illustratie meer natuurlijkheid en functionaliteit; bijvoorbeeld om het realistische gedrag van een kledingstuk uit te drukken of om een tekening te identificeren met een concrete stijl. Daarom vergelijken we het woord *pose* met *postuur*, van het Latijnse *positura*, dat verwijst naar een handeling of situatie. Om de correcte pose of houding te kiezen is het nodig om rekening te houden met factoren zoals de kledingstijl die het model draagt, om de bedoeling en de attitude vast te leggen. Wij hebben dit boek daarom onderverdeeld in drie hoofdstukken, waarin urban, *casual* en formele stijl aan bod komen, naast trucs, poses en de meest kenmerkende kledingstukken van die stijlen, die helpen om ze af te beelden: in eenvoudige lijnen en lichte tinten in aquarel worden de beste ontwerpen in het leven geroepen.

Urban Style

Style urbain

Urban Style

Urban stijl

Urban style emerged in cities as the result of a fusion of different cultures and lifestyles. Music styles like pop, hip hop, indie, and dancehall have led to an easily-distinguished urban fashion that is largely unaffected by ohter fashion trends. One of the major influences behind this look is 1980s skateboarding culture, a main feature of which is vintage sneakers. This casual look mixes sports clothes, loose T-shorts, open shirts, baggy or stovepipe pants, prints, caps, and hoodies, among others.

Le style urbain est celui qui naît dans les villes de la fusion entre les différentes cultures et les styles de vie. Les genres musicaux comme le pop, le *hip hop*, l'*indie* ou le *dancehall* ont créé une mode urbaine avec un style particulier, que l'on reconnaît facilement et qui est souvent en marge des tendances. La culture du *skateboard* dans les années quatre-vingt, dont les baskets *vintage* sont l'élément clé, constitue l'une des plus grandes influences de ce mode d'expression. Il s'agit d'un style informel qui allie vêtements de sport, tee-shirt larges, chemises ouvertes, pantalons larges ou fuselés, *prints*, casquettes, capuches… Pour le concevoir, il faut porter une attention toute particulière à l'attitude des mannequins et aux gestes typiques de ces sous-cultures.

Der Urban Style entsteht in den Städten aus der Verschmelzung verschiedener Kulturen und Lebensstile. Musikstile wie Pop, *hip hop*, *indie* oder *dancehall* haben eine urbane Mode mit eigenem Stil geschaffen, die leicht zu erkennen und in hohem Maße tendenzunabhängig ist. Einen großen Einfluss auf diese Ästhetik hatte die *skateboard*-Kultur der achtziger Jahre, zu deren Schlüsselelementen die *vintage*- Turnschuhe gehören. Es handelt sich um einen informellen Stilmix von Sportkleidung, weiten T-Shirts, offenen Hemden, weiten Hosen oder Röhrenjeans, *prints*, Mützen und Kapuzen …

De urban stijl is een stijl die ontstaan is in de grote steden, als gevolg van de samensmelting van verschillende culturen en levensstijlen. Muziekgenres zoals pop, *hip hop*, *indie* of *dancehall* hebben een urban mode voortgebracht met een eigen, zichzelf onderscheidende stijl, die zich in grote lijnen heeft losgemaakt van de trends. Een van de grootste invloeden op deze stijl is de *skateboard*-cultuur uit de jaren tachtig, met als sleutelelement *vintage* sportschoenen. Het gaat om een informele stijl, bestaande uit een mengeling van sportkleding, wijde shirts, open overhemden, wijde broeken of skinny jeans, *prints*, petten, capuchons… Om deze stijl te illustreren zijn de houding van de modellen en de voor deze subculturen kenmerkende gebaren belangrijk.

Military jacket with bodysuit and tracksuit pants

Veste militaire avec *body* et pantalon de survêtement

Jackett im Militärstil mit *body* und Jogginghose

Militair jasje met body en joggingbroek

Cotton T-shirt, overshirt with rolled up sleeves, and stove pipe pants

Tee-shirt en coton avec une veste aux manches retroussées et pantalon fuselé

Baumwoll-T-Shirt mit weitem Hemd mit aufgerollten Ärmeln und Röhrenhosen

Katoenen T-shirt met overhemd met opgestroopte mouwen en skinny broek

Hooded windbreaker and leggings

Coupe-vent à capuche et leggins

Windjacke mit Kapuze und *leggins*

Windjack met capuchon en legging

Leather jacket and jeans

Veste en cuir avec jean

Lederjacke mit Jeans

Leren jas met spijkerbroek

Checked shirt with denim vest and leggings

Chemise en flanelle avec veste en jean et leggins

Flanellhemd mit Jeansweste und *leggins*

Flanellen blouse met denim gilet en legging

Flannel shirt with rolled up sleeves, biker vest, and fitted pants

Chemise en flanelle avec les manches retroussées et veste moto avec pantalon ajusté

Flanellhemd mit aufgerollten Ärmeln, Bikerweste und enge Hose

Flanellen overhemd met opgestroopte mouwen, mouwloos Perfecto jasje en strakke broek

Sweater and jeans with wide belt

Pull et jean avec une ceinture large

Pullover und Jeans mit breitem Gürtel

Trui en jeans met brede riem

Sweater, jeans, and cap with earflaps

Pull et jean avec bonnet cache-oreille

Sweatshirt, Jeans und Ohrenklappenmütze

Sweater en spijkerbroek met pet met oorkleppen

Tank top, vest, and baggy pants

Débardeur avec gilet et pantalon *baggy*

Trägerhemd mit Weste und *baggy* Hose

Hemd met vestje en baggy broek.

Sweater with three-quarter sleeves, winter cap, and jeans

Pull manches trois quart avec un bonnet d'hiver et jean

Pullover mit halblangen Ärmeln, Wintermütze und Jeans

Trui met driekwartmouw, wintermuts en spijkerbroek

Hooded sports sweatshirt with leggings

Pull de sport à capuche et leggins

Sweatshirt mit Kapuze und *leggins*

Sportshirt met capuchon en legging

Long sleeve T-shirt, cap, and jeans

Tee-shirt à manches longues avec bonnet et jean

Langarm-T-Shirt, Mütze und Jeans

Shirt met lange mouw, muts en spijkerbroek

Hooded blouse with stand-up collar and
ruched pants

Blouse au col officier et à capuche et
pantalon avec un élastique sur le côté

Bluse mit geradem Ausschnitt mit Kapuze
und Hose mit seitlicher Gummi-Raffung

Blouse met rechte boord en capuchon en
broek met elastiek aan de zijkant

T-shirt, fitted jeans, and a Peruvian hat

Tee-shirt avec jean ajusté
et bonnet péruvien

T-Shirt mit engen Jeans und
peruanischer Mütze

T-shirt met strakke jeans
en Peruaanse muts

Cowl neck shirt with cap and low waist pants

Tee-shirt au col rond avec casquette et pantalon
taille basse

T-Shirt mit weitem Ausschnitt, Mütze und tief
sitzender Hose

T-shirt met wijde hals met pet en lage broek

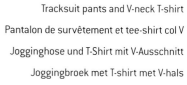

Tracksuit pants and V-neck T-shirt

Pantalon de survêtement et tee-shirt col V

Jogginghose und T-Shirt mit V-Ausschnitt

Joggingbroek met T-shirt met V-hals

Hooded sweatshirt and tracksuit pants

Pull à capuche et pantalon de survêtement

Sweatshirt mit Kapuze und Jogginghose

Sweatshirt met capuchon en joggingbroek

Denim jacket, tank top,
and tracksuit pants

Blouson en jean et débardeur
avec pantalon de survêtement

Jeansjacke und Träger-Shirt
mit Jogginghose

Spijkerjack en hemd
met joggingbroek

Checked shirt, pashmina, and leggings

Chemise à carreaux avec pashmina et *leggins*

Kariertes Hemd mit Pashmina-Schal und *leggins*

Geruite blouse met pashmina en legging

Rolled-up denim shirt with casual pants

Chemise en jean avec manches
retroussées et pantalon sport

Jeanshemd mit aufgerollten Ärmeln
und *sport* Hose

Denim overhemd met opgestroopte
mouwen en *sportieve* broek

Zip-up jacket with puff sleeves and
tracksuit pants

Pull de sport à manches princesse et
pantalon de survêtement

Sportlicher Pullover mit Prinzessärmeln
und Jogginghose

Sportieve sweater met
prinsessenmouwen en joggingbroek

Hooded sweatshirt and baggy
tracksuit pants

Pull à capuche et pantalon large
de survêtement

Sweatshirt mit Kapuze und
weiter Jogginghose

Sweatshirt met capuchon en
wijde joggingbroek

T-shirt dress with leggings

Robe tee-shirt avec *leggins*

T-Shirtkleid mit *leggins*

Blousejurk met legging

Work coveralls

Bleu de travail

Arbeits-Overall

Werkoverall

Beach dress

Robe de plage

Strandkleid

Strandjurk

Rolled-up summer pants with cotton T-shirt

Pantalon d'été retroussé et tee-shirt en coton

Aufgerollte Sommerhosen und Baumwoll-T-Shirt

Opgerolde zomerbroek met katoenen T-shirt

V-neck mini dress with ruffled sleeves combined with beret

Robe courte col V et manches à volants avec béret

Kurzes Kleid mit V-Ausschnitt und Volantärmeln und Baskenmütze

Korte jurk met V-hals en mouwen met ruches en baret

Matching jeans and denim jacket with checked shirt

Ensemble veste et pantalon en jean avec chemise à carreaux

Jeansanzug mit kariertem Hemd

Jeansset bestaand uit jasje en broek met geruit overhemd

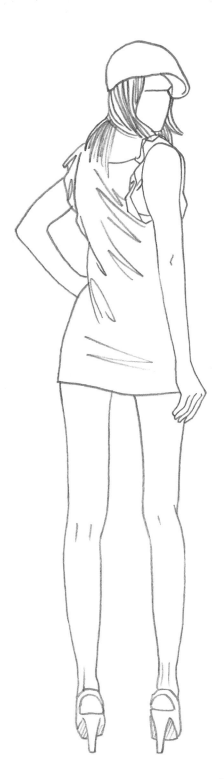

Wool coat with turtleneck dress

Manteau en laine avec robe à col roulé

Wollmantel und Kleid mit Rollkragen

Wollen jas met coljurk

Long sleeve T-shirt with pushed up sleeves, vest, neck scarf, and stovepipe pants

Tee-shirt à manches longues retroussées avec gilet, foulard autour du cou et pantalon slim

T-Shirt mit aufgerollten langen Ärmeln mit Weste, Halstuch und Röhrenhosen

T-shirt met lange, opgestrookte mouwen en gilet, sjaaltje om de nek en skinny broek

Hooded waterproof coat

Manteau imperméable à capuche

Regenmantel mit Kapuze

Regenjas met capuchon

T-shirt with rolled-up sleeves and
tight pants with cuffs

Tee-shirt manches retroussées et
pantalon ajusté à revers

T-Shirt mit aufgerollten Ärmeln und
enge Hosen mit Aufschlag

T-shirt met opgestrookte mouwen
en strakke broek met omgeslagen
onderkant

Mini dress worn with long scarf

Mini robe et écharpe longue autour du cou

Minikleid und langer Schal um den Hals

Mini-jurk en lange sjaal om de nek

Tank top, fingerless gloves, and
tracksuit pants

Débardeur avec gants sans doigts et
pantalon de survêtement

Träger-T-Shirt mit fingerlosen
Handschuhen und Jogginghose

Hemd met handschoenen zonder
vingers en joggingbroek

Short leather jacket and dress with tulip skirt

Veste courte en cuir avec robe boule

Kurze Lederjacke und Kleid mit Ballonrock

Kort leren jack met jurk met bolle rok

Varsity jacket with jeans

Veste avec pantalon de survêtement

Jacke mit Jogginghose

Jasje met joggingbroek

Tweed jacket with mini dress and leggings

Veste en *tweed* avec mini robe

tweed-Jackett mit Minikleid

Tweed jasje met mini-jurk

Polo shirt and jeans

Polo et jean

Polohemd und Jeans

Poloshirt en spijkerbroek

Casual style
Style casual
casual – Stil
Casual stijl

Casual is a form of dress that places emphasis on comfort and personal style. Jeans and T-shirts are considered the quintessential casual uniform. Sports clothing and 20th century spectator sports, together with different work uniforms, have has a significant influence on the casual style. Music, artistic currents, urban tribes, and other social groups have lent representative features which, combined with basic pieces, fit into the different looks of this style, such as a leather jacket, a cheesecloth *boho* dress, and a preppy cardigan, to name a few. Consideration should also be given to semi casual looks, which are closer to the formal style with the inclusion of blazers and suits. Drawing these looks can make use of relaxed or more sophisticated poses, depending on the combination of pieces, the influences they suggest, and what is being conveyed.

Le style *casual* est un *dress code* qui met l'accent sur le confort et l'expression personnelle. Le *jean* et le tee-shirt sont « l'uniforme *casual*» par excellence. Les vêtements sportifs, les différents sports de masse du 20e siècle ainsi que certaines tenues de travail ont largement influencé le style *casual*. Par ailleurs, la musique, les mouvements artistiques, les tribus urbaines et autres groupes sociaux ont apporté certains éléments représentatifs qui, combinés à des vêtements de base, conviennent aux *looks* de ce style, comme un blouson en cuir, une robe *boho*, un cardigan *preppy*, etc. N'oublions pas le *semi-casual*, qui ressemble au style formel mais inclut des *blazers*, des tailleurs, etc. Pour les dessiner, vous pouvez opter pour des poses décontractées ou plutôt sophistiquées, en fonction du choix des vêtements, de leur influence et ce que vous voulez transmettre.

Der *casual* -Stil ist ein *dress code*, der Komfort und Individualität betont. *Jeans* und T-Shirt bilden die «*casual*-Uniform» schlechthin. Die Sportkleidung und der Massensport des xx Jahrhunderts hatten ebenso wie bestimmte Arten von Arbeitskleidung einen großen Einfluss auf den *Casual*-Stil. Auf der anderen Seite haben Musik, künstlerische Strömungen, Jugendkultur und andere soziale Gruppen markante Elemente beigetragen, die, mit Basics kombiniert, zu den *Looks* dieses Stils passen, wie Lederjacken, *Boho*- Kleider aus Crash-Stoff, *Preppy* - Strickjacken, usw. Man sollte auch den *Semi-casual*- Stil beachten, der sich durch die Einbeziehung von *Blazern*, Anzügen, bzw. Kostümen, usw. dem formellen Stil annähert. Um sie zu zeichnen, kann man mit lässigen oder raffinierteren Posen spielen, abhängig von der Kombination der Kleidung, deren Einfluss auf diese Posen und davon, was man vermitteln will.

De *casual* stijl is de *dress code* waarin comfort en persoonlijke expressie vooraan staan. *Spijkerbroeken* en T-shirts worden gezien als het «*casual*-uniform» bij uitstek. Sportkleding en massasporten van de 20ste eeuw hebben, naast bepaalde werkkleding, grote invloed gehad op de *casual* stijl. Bovendien hebben muziek, kunststromingen, gangs en andere sociale groepen representatieve elementen met zich meegebracht die, gecombineerd met basics, in de *looks* van deze stijl passen, zoals het leren jack, de *boho* jurk, de *preppy* cardigan, etc. Aandacht verdient ook de *semi-casual* stijl, die in de buurt komt van de formele stijl met *blazers*, mantelpakjes, etc. Om deze te tekenen kan men spelen met nonchalante of juist geraffineerdere poses, afhankelijk van de kledingcombinatie, de invloed daarvan en van wat men wil overbrengen.

Ruffled dress, hat, and
cowboy boots

Robe à volants et chapeau
avec bottes santiag

Kleid mit Volants mit Hut
und Cowboystiefel

Strokenjurk en hoed
met cowboylaarzen

Fur coat and jeans

Manteau en cuir et jean

Felljacke und Jeans

Bontjas en spijkerbroek

Denim dress with asymmetrical close

Robe en jean avec fermeture croisée

Jeans-Wickelkleid

Denim jurk met gekruiste sluiting

Pea coat with hat and stovepipe pants

Manteau de marin avec chapeau et pantalon slim

Matrosenjacke mit Hut und Röhrenhosen

Zeemansjas met hoed en skinny broek

Blazer with large shoulders and mini dress

Veste à épaulettes et robe courte

Jackett mit Schulterpolstern und kurzem Kleid

Colbert met hoge schouders en korte jurk

Wool jacket with shirt, jeans, and boots

Veste en laine avec chemise et jean avec bottes

Wolljacke mit Hemd und Jeans mit Stiefeln

Wollen vest met overhemd, jeans en laarzen

Mini skirt and short sleeve shirt

Mini jupe avec chemisier à manches courtes

Minirock mit Kurzarmbluse

Minirok met T-shirt met korte mouw

Fitted suit

Costume cintré

Eng geschnittener Anzug

Strak kostuum

Bolero jacket with bodysuit and boyfriend cut pants

Veste boléro avec *body* et pantalon *boyfriend*

Bolerojacke mit *body* und boyfriend-Hose

Bolerojasje met body en *boyfriend* broek

Light jacket with fitted pants

Veste légère avec pantalon ajusté

Leichte Jacke mit enger Hose

Licht jasje met strakke broek

Mini dress with three-quarter sleeves and Mao collar

Robe courte à manches trois quart et col mao

Kurzes Kleid mit halblangen Ärmeln und Mao-Kragen

Korte jurk met driekwartmouw en Mao-boord

Shirt with rolled-up sleeves with shorts and trilby hat

Chemise aux manches retroussées avec *short* et chapeau trilby

Hemd mit aufgerollten Ärmeln, *shorts* und Trilby-Hut

Overhemd met opgestroopte mouwen, shorts en trilby-hoed.

Denim mini skirt

Robe en jean courte

Kurzes Jeanskleid

Korte denim jurk

Denim vest and stove pipe pants

Gilet en jean et pantalon slim

Jeansweste und Röhrenhose

Denim gilet en skinny broek

T-shirt, jeans, and tall boots

Tee-shirt et jean avec bottes hautes

T-Shirt und Jeans mit hohen Stiefeln

Shirt en spijkerbroek met hoge laarzen

Denim jacket with tight pants

Blouson en jean et pantalon ajusté

Jeansjacke und enge Hosen

Spijkerjack en strakke broek

Dress with puff sleeves and wide belt

Robe à manches princesse et ceinture large

Kleid mit Puffärmeln und breitem Gürtel

Jurk met pofmouwen en brede riem

Plain cotton T-shirt with
overshirt and dress shorts

Tee-shirt classique en coton
avec veste et bermuda

Basic-T-Shirt aus Baumwolle
und weites Hemd mit Bermudas

Katoenen basic T-shirt met
overhemd en bermuda

Long sleeve mini dress

Robe courte à manches longues

Kurzes Kleid mit langen Ärmeln

Korte jurk met lange mouwen

Fitted suit worn with neck scarf

Costume cintré et foulard autour du cou

Eng geschnittener Anzug mit Seidentuch

Strak pak met foulard om de nek

Mini dress with leather vest

Robe courte avec gilet en cuir

Kurzes Kleid mit Lederweste

Korte jurk met leren gilet

Blazer and jeans with
scarf and mittens

Veste et pantalon en jean
avec écharpe et moufles

Sakko und Jeans mit Schal
und Fäustlingen

Colbert en spijkerbroek
met sjaal en wanten

Turtleneck dress with three quarter sleeves

Robe courte à manches trois quart et à col roulé

Kleid mit Prinzessärmeln und Rollkragen

Jurk met driekwartmouw en col

Three quarter length army coat with shirt and jeans

Manteau militaire ¾ avec chemise et jean

¾ langer Militärmantel (Parka) mit Hemd und Jeans

Militaire driekwartjas met overhemd en spijkerbroek

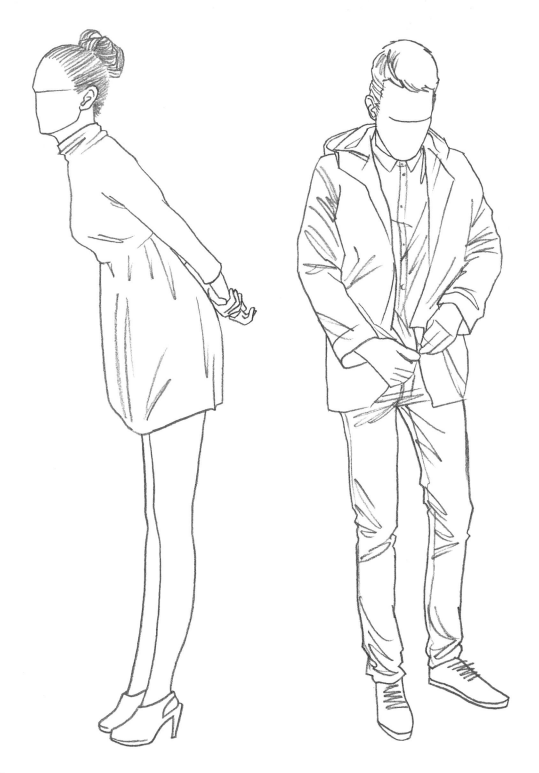

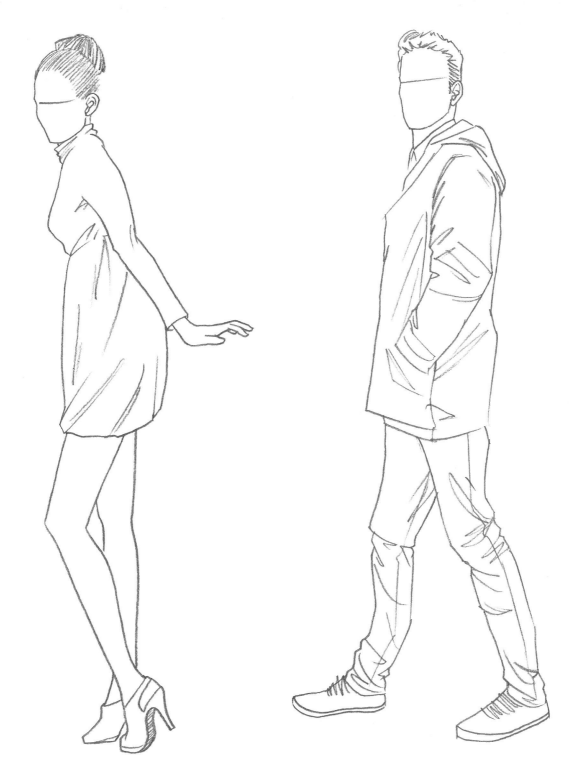

Coat, mini dress, and leggings

Manteau avec mini robe et *leggins*

Jackett mit Minikleid und *leggins*

Jas met mini-jurk en legging.

Three quarter length coat with
scarf, hat, and tight pants

Manteau ¾ avec écharpe,
chapeau et pantalon ajusté

¾ Mantel mit Schal, Hut
und engen Hosen

Driekwartjas met sjaal,
hoed en strakke broek

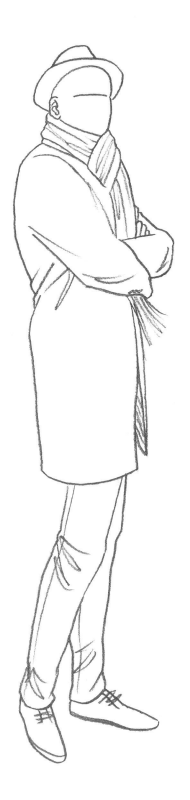

Sequined jacket with mini dress and leggings

Veste à paillettes avec mini robe et *leggins*

Jackett mit Pailletten, Minikleid und *leggins*

Paillettenjasje met mini-jurk en legging

Biker jacket with cotton T-shirt and straight-leg pants

Blouson moto avec tee-shirt en coton et pantalon droit

Bikerjacke mit Baumwoll-T-Shirt und gerader Hose

Perfecto jasje met katoenen T-shirt en rechte broek

20s-style mini fringe dress

Robe courte à franges style années vingt

Kurzes Zwanzigerjahre-Kleid mit Fransen

Korte jaren twintig jurk met franjes

Shirt and vest with classic pants

Chemise et gilet avec pantalon classique

Hemd und Weste mit klassischer Hose

Overhemd en gilet met klassieke broek

Strapless dress

Robe bustier

Bandeau- Kleid

Strapless jurk

Silk bomber jacket with baggy pants

Veste aviateur en soie et pantalon *baggy*

bomber Jacke aus Seide mit *baggy* Hose

Zijden bomber-jasje met baggy broek

Shirt dress with short vest

Robe chemise avec gilet court

Hemdblusenkleid mit kurzer Weste

Overhemdjurk met kort gilet

Shirt with rolled-up sleeves, 4-button double-breasted vest, and cotton pants

Chemise manches retroussées avec gilet croisé à quatre boutons et pantalon en coton

Hemd mit aufgerollten Ärmeln und Weste mit vier Knöpfen und Baumwollhose

Overhemd met opgestroopte mouwen en gekruist gilet met vier knopen en katoenen broek

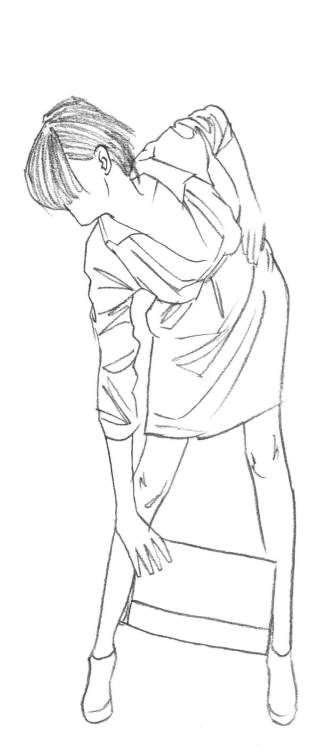

Fur coat with fitted pants

Manteau en cuir avec pantalon ajusté

Felljacke mit enger Hose

Bontjas met strakke broek

Summer suit

Costume d'été

Sommeranzug

Zomerkostuum

Strapless dress with sash belt

Robe bustier avec ceinture large

Bandeau- Kleid mit Schärpe

Strapless jurk met sjerp

Leather jacket with tight pants

Blouson en cuir et pantalon ajusté

Lederjacke und enge Hosen

Leren jack en strakke broek

Shirt and draped skirt

Chemise avec jupe drapée

Bluse mit gerafftem Rock

Blouse met gedrapeerde rok

Classic suit with shirt

Costume classique avec chemise

Klassischer Anzug mit Hemd

Klassiek kostuum met overhemd

Tank top and bubble skirt

Débardeur et jupe boule

Top mit Spaghettiträgern und Ballonrock

Top met bandjes en ballonrok

Coat, jeans, and boots

Manteau et jean avec bottes hautes

Mantel und Jeans mit Stiefeln

Jas en spijkerbroek met laarzen

Draped mini dress with sweetheart neckline

Robe courte drapée avec décolleté en cœur

Kurzes gerafftes Bustierkleid

Korte gedrapeerde jurk met hartvormig decolleté

Blazer, fine knit sweater, and tight pants

Veste avec pull en maille fine et pantalon ajusté

Jackett mit Feinstrickpullover und engen Hosen

Colbert met trui van dunne tricot en strakke broek

Formal style
Style formel
Formeller Stil
Formele stijl

Formal style can generally be defined as clothes that are suitable for social events. The use of black and white looks one of the standards in the formal social wardrobe. Depending on importance of the event, tuxedos, morning suits, and white tie for men, and evening gowns and cocktail dresses for women are internationally accepted. However, except on occasions requiring strict etiquette, semi-formal (between casual and formal) is currently a socially acceptable look. This features pieces that respond to the canons of style laid down by movie icons such as Audrey Hepburn's little black dress, Agent 007's suits of impeccable British tailoring, and Bogart's trench coat and fedora. Drawing this style should involve more serene and elegant poses with predominantly black and white looks.

Le style formel se définit en général comme la tenue appropriée pour les événements sociaux. Le look blanc et noir est un classique de la tenue sociale formelle. Selon le degré d'importance, le smoking, la jaquette ou le frac pour l'homme et la robe de soirée pour la femme seraient les tenues de référence internationales. Cependant, de nos jours dans le monde de la mode, sauf lorsque le protocole l'exige, le style à moitié formel (entre le casual et le formel) est accepté. Certaines tenues répondent aux canons d'élégance et sont des icônes du grand écran comme la petite robe noire d'Audrey Hepburn, l'impeccable costume british de l'agent 007 ou la gabardine et le chapeau borsalino de Bogart. Pour représenter ce style, nous opterons pour des poses plutôt sereines et élégantes, privilégiant le look en noir et blanc.

Der formelle Stil gilt allgemein als die angemessene Kleidung für gesellschaftliche Anlässe. Der Gebrauch von Looks in schwarz und weiß ist Standard in der formellen Gesellschaftskleidung. Je nach Bedeutung des Anlasses ist der Smoking, der Cutaway oder der Frack für den Herrn und das Abend- oder Cocktailkleid für die Dame, der internationalen Etikette entsprechend, angemessen. Jedoch wird in der heutigen Mode, außer zu protokollarischen Anlässen, eine weniger strenge Etikette und ein semiformeller Stil (zwischen casual und formell) akzeptiert, bei dem Kleidungsstücke, die zum Eleganz-Kanon gehören, so z.B. Kino-Ikonen wie das little black dress („das kleine Schwarze") von Audrey Hepburn, der british makellose Maßanzug des Agenten 007 oder Bogarts Trenchcoat und Borsalino. Um diesen Stil zu zeichnen, entscheiden wir uns für ruhigere und elegante Posen, bei denen Looks in schwarz-weiß vorherrschen.

Deze stijl wordt, in algemene bewoordingen, omschreven als de geschikte kleding voor sociale gelegenheden. Het gebruik van looks in wit en zwart is een standaard van sociaal formele kleding. Bovenaan het referentiekader van de internationale etiquette staan de smoking, jacquet of het rokkostuum voor mannen en de avondjurk of cocktailjurk voor vrouwen. In het huidige modebeeld is echter, behalve bij gelegenheden waar het protocol vereist is, het gebruik van 'medium' etiquette en een semi-formele stijl (tussen casual en formeel in) toegestaan. Daaronder vallen kledingstukken die overeenkomen met de canons van elegantie, waaronder filmiconen zoals de little black dress van Audrey Hepburn, het onberispelijke British mantelpak van agent 007, of de gabardine en de borsalino van Bogart. Om deze stijl te tekenen kiezen we voor beheerste en elegantere poses, waar witte en zwarte looks overheersen.

Cotton sweater and classic pants

Pull en coton et pantalon classique

Baumwollpullover und klassische Hose

Katoenen trui en klassieke broek

Fusion of blazer/coat with straight-leg
pants and boots

Ensemble veste-jaquette avec pantalon
droit et bottes

Jackett/Cutaway mit gerader
Hose und Stiefeln

Colbert/jacquet-combinatie met rechte
broek en laarzen

Strapless baggy jumpsuit

Salopette bustier baggy

baggy trägerloser Overall

Strapless baggy overall

Cardigan and neck tie with straight-leg
pants and travel bag

Cardigan et cravate avec pantalon
droit et sac de voyage

Strickjacke und Krawatte, gerade
Hose und Reisetasche

Gebreid vestje en stropdas met
rechte broek en reistas

Shirt, mini skirt, and elastic belt

Chemise avec jupe courte et
ceinture élastique

Bluse mit kurzem Rock und
elastischem Gürtel

Blouse met korte rok en elastische riem

Matching vest and pants

Ensemble deux pièces gilet et pantalon

Zweiteiliger Anzug, bestehend aus
Weste und Hose

Tweedelig pak van gilet en broek

Cutaway jacket and mini dress

Cardigan avec mini robe

Gehrock mit Minirock

Jacquet met mini-jurk

Three quarter length wool coat with shirt
and cotton pants

Manteau en laine ¾ avec chemise et
pantalon en coton

¾ Mantel aus Wolle mit Hemd und
Baumwollhose

Wollen driekwartjas met overhemd en
katoenen broek

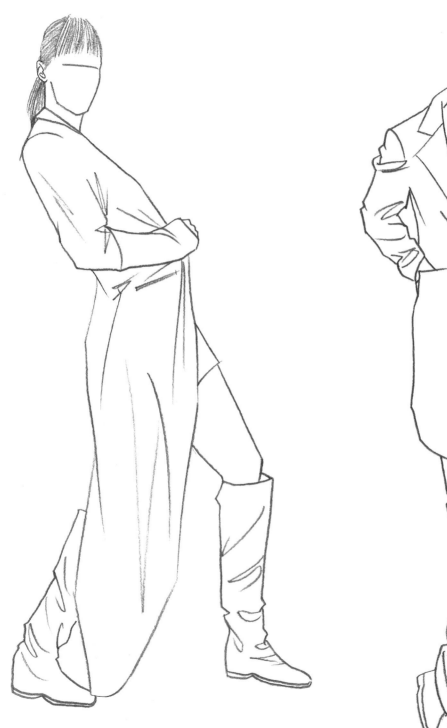

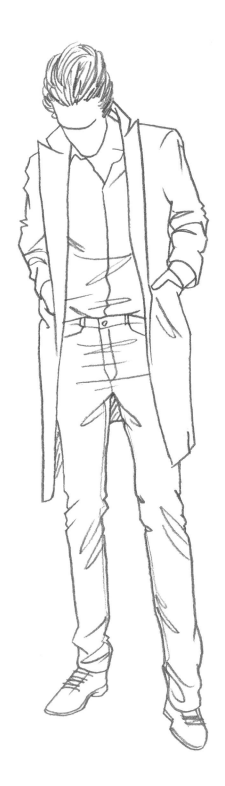

Dress with ruffled sleeves and sash belt

Robe à manches à volants et ceinture large

Kleid mit Volantärmel und Schärpe

Jurk met mouwen met ruches en sjerp

Shirt and tie with fitted pants

Chemise et cravate avec pantalon ajusté

Hemd und Krawatte mit enger Hose

Overhemd en stropdas met strakke broek

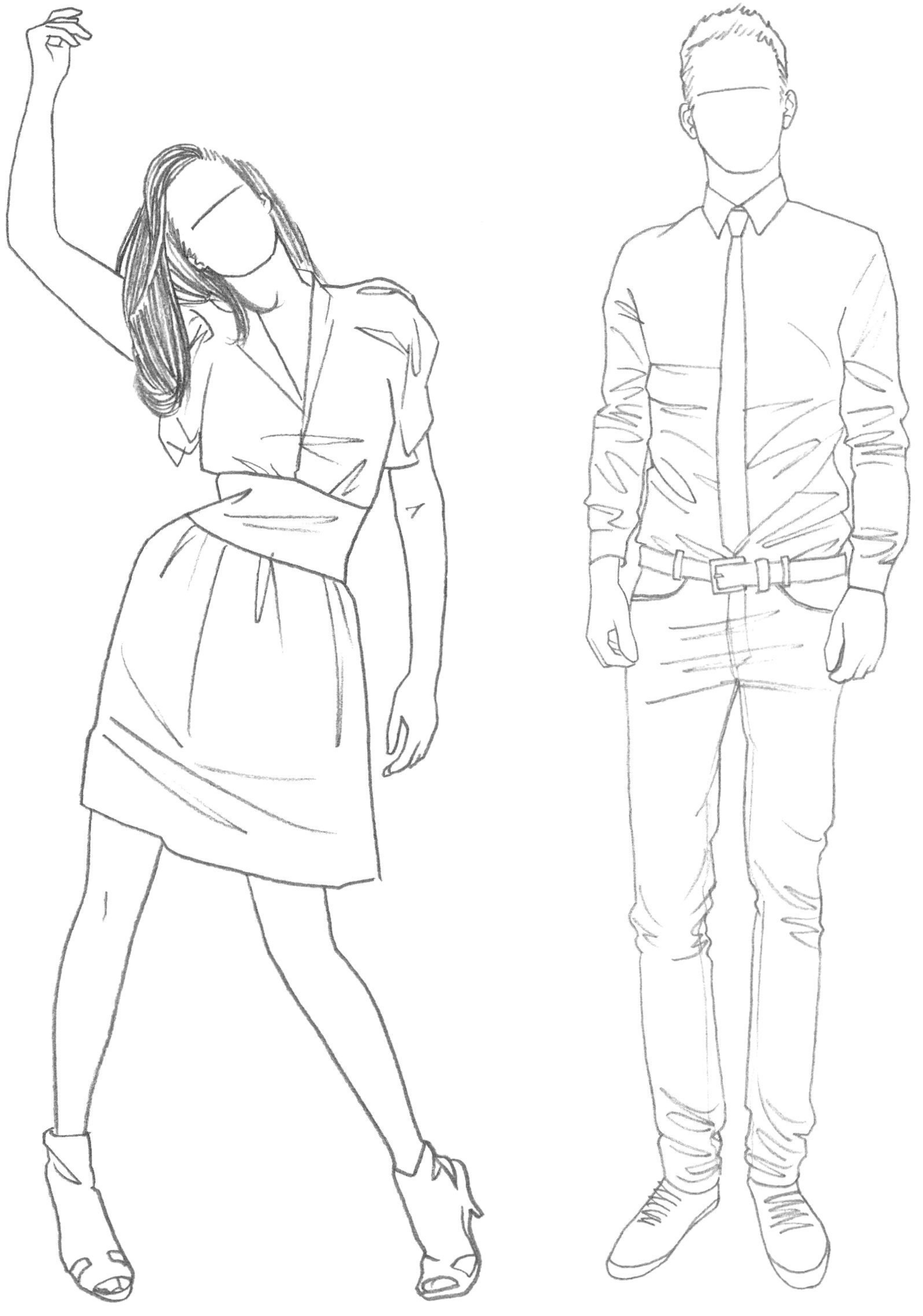

Mini dress with leg of mutton sleeves

Robe courte à manches bouffantes

Kurzes Kleid mit Keulenärmel

Korte jurk met pofmouw

Printed vest with classic pants

Gilet de costume fantaisie avec
pantalon classique

Phantasieweste mit klassischer Hose

Fantasiegilet met klassieke broek

Strapless pant dress

Robe combinaison bustier

Trägerloses Hosenkleid

Strapless broekjurk

50s-style leather biker jacket with shirt and tight pants

Blouson de moto en cuir des années cinquante avec chemise et pantalon ajusté

Fünfzigerjahre-Motorradjacke aus Leder mit Hemd und enger Hose

Leren jaren vijftig motorjack met overhemd en strakke broek

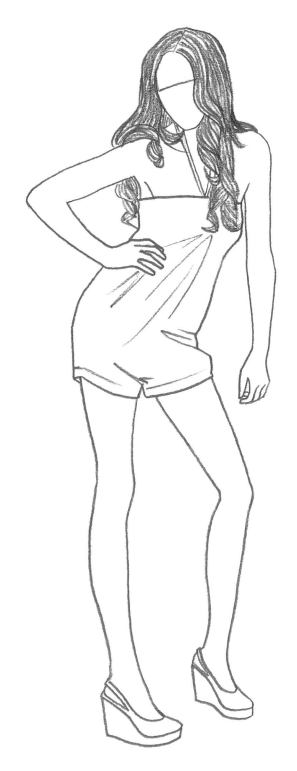

V-neck dress and sash belt

Robe avec col en V et ceinture intégrée sous la poitrine

Kleid mit V-Ausschnitt und Schärpe

V-halsjurk met sjerp/ceintuur

Shirt with bow tie, sweater, and tight pants

Chemise et pull avec nœud papillon et pantalon ajusté

Hemd und Pullover mit Fliege und engen Hosen

Overhemd en trui met vlinderdasje en strakke broek

Bolero jacket with classic dress

Veste boléro avec robe classique

Bolero-Jacke mit klassischem Kleid

Bolerojasje met klassieke jurk

Three quarter length wool coat with classic pants

Manteau ¾ en laine avec pantalon classique

¾ Mantel aus Wolle mit klassischer Hose

Wollen driekwartjas met klassieke broek

Sleeveless mini dress with stand-up collar

Robe courte à col officier sans manches

Kurzes ärmelloses Kleid mit geradem Ausschnitt

Mouwloze korte jurk met rechte hals

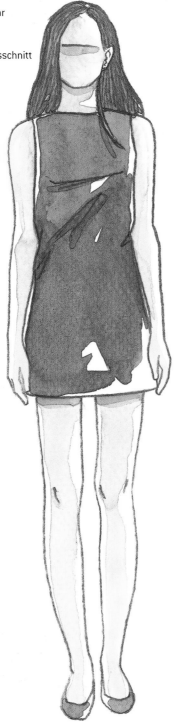

Suit and three quarter length coat

Costume avec manteau ¾

Anzug mit 3/4 Mantel

Pak met driekwartjas

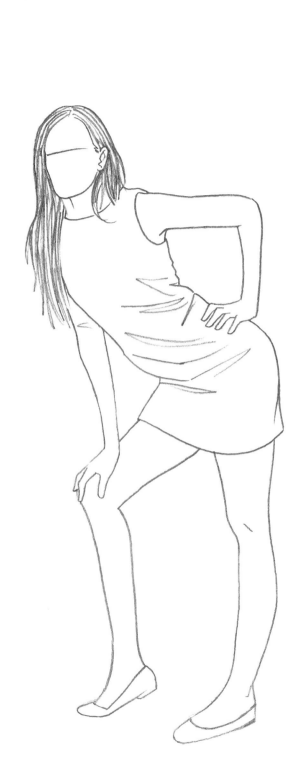

Long trench coat with wide belt and leggings

Gabardine longue avec ceinture large et leggins

Langer Regenmantel mit breitem Gürtel und leggins

Lange regenjas met brede riem en legging

Trench coat with shirt, tie, jeans, and beret

Gabardine avec chemise, cravate, pantalon et béret

Regenmantel mit Hemd und Krawatte, Jeans und Schiebermütze

Regenjas met overhemd, stropdas en spijkerbroek met baret

Mini dress and short jacket with wide neck

Mini robe et veste courte avec col en U

Minikleid und kurzes Jackett mit U-förmigem
Ausschnitt

Mini-jurk en kort jasje met U-vormige hals

Suit with trilby hat

Costume avec chapeau type trilby

Anzug mit Trilby-Hut

Pak met trilby-hoed

Dress with bell sleeves and boat neck

Robe à manches larges et col bateau

Kleid mit weiten Ärmeln und U-Boot-Ausschnitt

Jurk met wijde mouwen en boothals

Casual suit

Costume sport

sport-Anzug

Sportief pak

Dress with low neckline and belt

Robe col échancré et ceinture

Kleid mit tiefem Ausschnitt und Gürtel

Jurk met diep decolleté en riem

Six-button three quarter length coat
with straight-leg pants

Veste technologique et pantalon slim

Techno-Jacke und Röhrenhosen

Techno-jas en skinny broek

Long dress with sweetheart neckline

Robe longue avec décolleté en cœur

Langes Bustierkleid

Lange jurk met hartvormig decolleté

Dress suit

Costume de cérémonie

Abendanzug

Avondkostuum